The real Joan of Arc?

A History Mystery

by

Terry Deary

Illustrations by Linda Birch

W
FRANKLIN WATTS
LONDON • NEW YORK • SYDNEY

Contents

The real
Joan of Arc?

To Eleanor Rowley-Conwy

First published in 1996 by Franklin Watts

This paperback edition published in 1997

Franklin Watts
96 Leonard Street
London
EC2A 4RH

Franklin Watts Australia
14 Mars Road
Lane Cove
NSW 2006

Series editor: Paula Borton
Designer: Sally Boothroyd

A CIP catalogue record for this book
is available from the British Library.

ISBN 0 7496 2620 8 (pbk)
0 7496 2180 X (hbk)

Dewey Classification 942.03

Printed in Great Britain

Introduction

History is full of mysteries. Stories are passed down through the years and most of us believe them simply because they are written in books. But sometimes the writers get it wrong! History writers have been known to:

- make mistakes
- exaggerate
- invent 'facts'
- leave out important facts
- tell whopping great lies

This makes your job of understanding the past very tricky.

What is the truth? Who is telling it?

When a detective sets out to discover the truth he may have to solve a mystery. He must ask questions and work out who is lying and who is telling the truth. In this book that's just what you have to do. Become a history detective.

You will be given some fascinating facts mixed with some fascinating lies. Sort them out and solve the mystery. This *History Mystery* is arranged in three parts:

Part One

To make the mystery more enjoyable to read, it has been re-told in the form of a story. Imagine yourself in the shoes of two young detectives. Travel back in time to discover how they uncover the evidence.

Part Two

To help you understand the world in which the mystery is set, there is then a selection of facts about the people of those days and their lives. Some of these facts will help you solve the mystery, others are simply fascinating facts on their own.

Part Three

Finally the story ends with the characters reaching their own 'solution' to the problem. You might not agree with their solution – some historians would certainly disagree! But remember . . . it is *a* solution, not *the* solution. In history there is hardly ever such a thing as *the one* right answer. That's why history is so strange and irritating and enjoyable and infuriating. History is a mystery . . . and *that's* a fact!

Part One

The Story of Jeanne the Maid

1

I left behind the great grey walls of my monastery. It was the first time in six years that I'd been outside those walls and the sky looked like a huge silver-blue bowl over the earth.

The road was dusty and the road was dangerous, as miserable Brother Michael had reminded me. "When you reach the forests there are robbers who will cut your throat for a penny," he smirked.

"But I don't have a penny. I'm a monk," I told him.

"Then they'll cut your throat for fun," he said.

"God will be with me," I said.

"Then I hope he has his sword with him," Michael muttered.

I was still a long way from the forests. The fields and the villages seemed friendly enough. But the heat of the sun made me sweat in my woollen habit and my sandals began to rub a blister on my foot.

When I stopped at a well in a village square a woman offered me bread and cheese in exchange for a prayer for her dead husband.

"Where am I?" I asked.

"This is Domremy village," she said. She also offered me some ointment for my foot. "You're not used to walking, then," she said as she wrapped some linen over the sore spot.

"No," I sighed and rubbed my aching legs. "My parents sent me to the monastery when I was seven. I've never left it since. But the abbot wants a message taking to Orleans." I patted my leather wallet that hung from a strap on my shoulder. "He said I'm old enough to deliver it for him."

"It will be dark in an hour," the woman said. "You shouldn't be on the roads after dark. I'd offer you a room myself," she said, "but my house is too poor, brother."

"I'm not a brother yet," I told her. "I'm only a novice."

She nodded. "There is a farm at the end of the village, on the Orleans road," she said. "That would make a more suitable resting place for a young monk."

"Why?" I asked.

"You will see," she said and gave me directions. I thanked her and she repeated her warning. "Don't be on the road after sunset."

I limped through the village and past its castle. The road was dry and rutted, uncomfortable to walk on, and I longed to see the farm the woman had described. When I

-11-

reached it the shadows were long and the air was still. Not even the birds sang there.

Crops grew in the fields but they were parched and full of weeds. The house itself was built of stone, not like the cottages of the peasants. It had once been fine, but now the shutters hung from broken hinges and the darkened windows stared out like blind eyes. No one cared.

I walked into a yard that was a cobbled square formed by the house and three barns. From somewhere a pair of eyes watched me as I hobbled to the farmhouse door.

My knock sounded hollow and it echoed down empty passages. "They're in the kitchen at the back," the voice said. I swung round and peered into the deep shadow of the barn door. One shadow, paler than the rest, moved towards me. As it came into the light in the centre of the weed-choked yard I saw it was a girl. She clutched some hens' eggs to her.

"Good evening," I said.

"What you want then?" she asked, sauntering towards me. She was a year or so younger than me, maybe eleven or twelve. She was also the dirtiest creature I had ever seen. In the monastery we bathed once a month even if we didn't need to. This girl looked as if she had never seen a bath. Her hair was as tangled as a thorn bush and bleached by the sun.

"I was looking for shelter," I said.

She gave a sharp jerk of the head as a signal to follow her and walked round the side of the house. She marched through a back door and announced me. "Young novice wants a bed," she said abruptly.

The people at the kitchen table stopped eating and looked at me as I followed the girl into the room. There were three men at the table, peasant workers, and they were scraping at their wooden bowls with wooden spoons. It was the woman who stood by the fireplace that caught my eye.

She was tall and as pale as the girl was sun-browned. Her face was as sad and lovely as the pictures of Mary in the monastery chapel, but her eyes were deep as a well.

"I've been sent by my abbot to Orleans. I was hoping you could offer me shelter," I said. Four pairs of hollow eyes stared back at me.

"Ellie," the mistress of the house said to the girl, "he must stay in the barn tonight."

"What?" the girl said, uncomfortable. "That barn?"

"Brother," the woman said, turning to me, "young Ellie will cook some of her eggs for your supper. This stew is not fit for a monk." She scooped up some of the cauldron liquid in her ladle and let it fall back.

The girl showed me the way to the barn, then stood at the doorway, suddenly afraid. "The straw's soft in there," she said. "I'll bring your supper soon – I'll leave it at the door."

"What's wrong with the place?" I asked. She was no

longer the bold child I'd met at first. She refused to look me in the eye.

"Nothing," she said. "You'll be all right." And ran off before I could ask what she meant.

I waited for her to return. She didn't. Instead the mistress of the house arrived with the eggs, bread and a jug of wine.

"Thank you," I said. "I will pray for you," I promised.

She looked at me in silence for a while then spoke in a soft, low voice. "You are on the road to Orleans?" she said.

I nodded, "Yes, madame."

"Then I'd like you to do something for me while you are there."

"Yes, madame?"

"I want you to find my daughter."

2

Madame du Lys began to speak quickly and nervously. She seemed afraid of being overheard. "We called her Jeannette at home but everyone else called her Jeanne. When she left home she called herself Jeanne the Maid. Perhaps you've heard of her?"

"Yes, madame," I said. Even in the monastery everyone had heard of Jeanne the Maid. There were endless arguments about the girl. But that had all been ten years ago. Jeanne the Maid was dead. Everyone knew that.

"My husband died last month. My sons have left home. Even my younger daughter, Catherine, has gone. If my Jeanne is still alive I want to see her again."

"Of course, madame," I muttered. Maybe the woman was crazy, I thought. I'd heard that unhappiness can do that to people.

"Jeanne was always . . . different to the other children in the village. When she was thirteen she began to hear her 'voices'. She didn't tell anyone about them, of course. St Margaret, St Catherine and St Michael they were. They came to her while she was sitting here and gave her messages from heaven."

I shivered and looked around the bleak barn. There was nothing here grand enough for angels. But, Madame du Lys reminded me, "Jesus was born in a stable. Angels

visited him there."

"Of course," I replied.

"They told Jeanne that she had to become a soldier and drive the English armies out of France. They told her she had to have Prince Charles crowned King of France in Reims. My Jeanne tried to tell her voices it was impossible for a young girl to do such things. They said that with God behind her anything was possible. After three years she obeyed the voices."

"She became a soldier? Just like that?" I asked.

"Ah, no. At first she needed a powerful helper – one on earth, you understand. She decided to go to Vaucouleurs to ask for the help of Robert de Baudricourt, the king's chief officer for this region. She needed a guard to travel to see the prince – she needed a horse and she needed money."

"You let her go?" I asked.

Madame du Lys frowned. "We didn't know. Jeanne persuaded my cousin, Durand, to take her. He came to us and lied. He said he wanted Jeanne to help in his house while his wife was ill. Then he took her off to Vaucouleurs. She was gone before her father or I could stop her." The tall woman sighed and looked up to the roof that was black with bats. "That was more than ten years ago. After a hundred years of fighting, the English are almost gone and the Prince has been crowned king, just as Jeanne's voices promised. But they also told her she would die."

I remembered the story myself. The English captured her in battle. They put her on trial as a witch . . . then they burned her. "What makes you think she may be alive?" I asked gently.

"Stories. Stories from Orleans. They say she has

–16–

appeared there. My sons went to see. They say it is Jeanne."

"Is it a miracle?" I whispered. The young novices at my monastery were taught the lives of the saints. I knew about miracles, although I had never seen one. "Has she risen from the dead?"

The woman shrugged. "Perhaps. Or perhaps the English didn't burn her after all. Maybe they burned someone else and let my Jeanne go free."

"Why would they do that?"

"Who knows?" she said, "who knows?" She sighed, "When you are in Orleans you may find out something. If it is Jeanne – and if she is alive – tell her to come home."

She took the lantern away and left me in darkness. I woke in the middle of the night to pray as I'd done at two o'clock each morning for the past six years. Nothing would break the habit.

No angels visited me that night and there were no 'voices'. Only the rustling of bats above my head and the squeaking of rats in the straw.

I woke again at first light. A voice from the doorway said, "There's some food for you." The scruffy girl was watching me.

"Can you bring it in, please?" I asked.

She shook her head violently. "I wouldn't go in there for a hundred pounds," she said.

"You've heard about the angels," I said.

As I stepped forward to take the plate of gruel the girl leaned against the doorpost. "Madame du Lys is going mad, you know. Just like her daughter."

"You couldn't have known Jeanne the Maid," I said. "That all happened ten years ago."

"My mother knew her. Mother said Jeanne left Domremy to escape from a scandal."

"That's not what everyone else says," I argued.

"I don't care what everyone else says," she sniffed.

"Jeanne was engaged to be married to a young man. Then she broke off the engagement. She changed her mind. He took her to court but she got away with it. Mother said Jeanne went off dressed like a man. That's evil. That's why the English burned her when they caught her. Mother says it served her right."

I ate the gruel. It was thin and watery. No one seemed to care much at this house.

"Jeanne's brothers are worse than her. As soon as she became famous they rushed off to join her. Made a lot of money just for being her brothers."

"They took a share of her fame, did they?" I asked.

"They didn't take a share of her flames though, did they?" the girl said bitterly. She looked straight at me with her fierce dark eyes. "Take me with you. I hate it here."

I caught my breath. "It's not . . . proper for a monk to be in the company of a woman," I said. I repeated what Brother Michael used to say. It was something in the Bible: "All the wickedness in the world is small compared to the wickedness of a woman."

"Hah!" Ellie snorted as she stormed off across the yard. "It wasn't women who burned Jeanne the Maid."

"If anyone did," I thought as I set off for Vaucouleurs. I was determined to find out the truth and Robert de Baudricourt could probably help.

"Take me with you," the girl shouted after me.

"No."

3

The sky grew smaller as the road ran into the woods. A light breeze stirred the trees and their dry brown whispers made me nervous. I waited for the thieves and cut-throats to jump out from behind every trunk. When the forest was at its deepest and darkest I turned quickly and saw a figure vanish into the trees. So I wasn't imagining it.

I knew I couldn't outrun them, but thought I might be able to out-think them. I pretended I'd seen nothing. The next time the road took a turn, and I was out of their sight for a few moments, I dived off the path into the forest, crouched in the undergrowth and waited.

I only had to wait a minute. The figure was small, thin . . . and familiar. "Ellie!" I called from my hiding place.

She gave a small scream, turned and placed her hands on her hips. She glared at me as I walked back to the path. "What you want to scare me like that for?" she demanded.

"I wanted to know who was following me," I said.

"Only me," she shrugged and stirred the dust of the road with her thin shoe.

"But . . ."

"I'm going with you," she interrupted. "You need a guide. Someone to look after you."

That was true, but she didn't seem like a very powerful bodyguard. "Thank you," I said. "But you'd better go back."

She looked at me with wide and worried eyes. I noticed she'd cleaned her face. "I'm never going back," she said. "If I stay there my mum will marry me off to one of the peasants when I'm twelve. That's next year. I want to see the world. You know what they say, 'Town air makes men free.' People in towns aren't tied to the land."

"Ellie, you were born to be a land-working peasant. That's God's will. It is a sin to oppose it."

"God doesn't have to marry filthy Jacques," she said and stamped down the road ahead of me trailing clouds of dust.

To be honest, Ellie made a good companion as well as a useful one. She was curious about everything. "What's in your leather bag?" she asked.

"A letter for the abbot and a precious relic," I told her.

"What's a relic?" she asked.

"A rare and precious piece of history. I have a bone from St Anthony's arm," I said.

"Give me a look," she demanded.

Carefully, reverently, I pulled the ancient bone from my leather bag. Ellie looked at it closely and sniffed. She looked as if she was going to say something then changed her mind.

With our chatter I forgot about the gloomy threat of the forest. By evening we'd arrived at the castle of Vaucouleurs.

The gates were open and soldiers were drilling in the courtyard. They all wore rich red tunics. "That's Duke Robert's livery. Some peasants join his army just to get the free clothes," Ellie told me.

We crossed the courtyard and Ellie walked up to a soldier resting against the wall. "Where will we find his lordship, my man?" Ellie demanded.

The man blinked, scowled at the girl, then a crafty expression crept over his face. "He's in the Great Hall.

Having his dinner . . . my lady."

"Then we'll go and see him," Ellie announced grandly.

The man gave a small smile. "Go straight ahead at the top of the stairs," he smirked.

We climbed the stone stairway and I was almost into its dark mouth when I heard the dog growl. A yellow dog with white foam dripping from its snarling mouth. I'll swear its eyes glowed like hot metal.

I began to back towards the stairs and muttered a fast prayer as the growl grew in its throat. I bumped into Ellie and warned her to get back.

She pushed past me and held out a hand. "Here, dog!" she said and threw something white towards it. The beast snapped it and began to chew happily.

We walked past the dog towards the doors. "What did you give it?"

"A bone," she said.

"A bone! Where on earth did you get a bone?" I laughed.

"Out of your leather bag," she said.

I stopped laughing and started choking. "St . . . St . . . Anthony's armbone! It was a saint's relic. It was priceless. The holiest thing in France!"

"It was a lamb's bone," Ellie said. "I didn't want to tell you," she shrugged and pushed the door open. I was still shaking with the horror and confusion as she pulled me into the Great Hall. I stumbled over the rushes on the floor. Rich, colourful tapestries hung from the walls and the Duke and his followers talked loudly as they ate.

The babble of noise shocked me. All monastery meals were held in silence. I'd had to learn about a hundred hand signals in order to ask my brothers for things at meal times.

Duke Robert was even fatter than Brother Michael. He was chewing at a large bird that could have been a swan. "Who are you?" he snarled, as vicious as his guard dog.

Ellie stepped forward boldly. "My lord, we have a visitor. Brother John from a Benedictine monastery," she announced.

"I've got a priest," he said. "I don't need another."

"I don't want a position in your household, thank you," I said. "I was hoping you might give me some information."

"I thought you monks knew everything," he said.

I waited quietly and patiently for the duke and his friends to finish laughing at his joke. Finally I said, "I hoped you would tell me about the girl called Jeanne."

The eaters went quiet and stared at me. "Sit down," Robert de Baudricourt said and made a space next to him at the top table.

4

"Do you know what I did when Jeanne the Maid came and asked me for an introduction to Prince Charles?" Robert de Baudricourt asked.

"Sent her with a guard to the prince in Chinon?" I guessed.

"I sent her home. I sent her packing, back to Domremy with her little uncle. A sixteen-year-old girl in a poor red dress. What could she do that the power of the French army had failed to do? It was a joke," he growled. "But people in France got to hear about the girl and her 'voices'. They wanted to see her. The prince decided that nothing would be lost by letting her try. If she killed her foolish self then it didn't really matter. The stubborn little vixen came back a month or so after I'd thrown her out. This time we decided to let her go to the prince."

"You didn't believe in her miracles then?" I asked.

"Miracles are for monks. Cold steel is for a soldier like me," he said. "We gave her an escort of armed men and a horse. Her uncle brought her men's clothes so she could ride in disguise. We cropped her hair and packed her off. I thought that would be the last I'd see of her. She was small – strong, for a girl, but no taller than you, boy."

Duke Robert took a long drink of wine from his goblet and wiped his mouth on the back of his hand.

A knight at the end of the table leaned forward. He called across the table to the duke, "Miracles? Yes there were miracles. That's what a monk wants to hear about, isn't it?

First it was a miracle that she persuaded an old fool like you to support her."

Robert de Baudricourt laughed. "All right, all right. I will tell Brother John about Jeanne the Maid's so-called miracles – but he must make up his own mind about the truth of them. I mean to say, have you heard that story about her finding the prince in disguise?"

I shook my head. Robert de Baudricourt carved a slice from a joint of beef and chewed it as he explained. "When she reached Chinon it took some weeks for her to get to see the prince, you understand. When she was finally given permission, the story goes that Charles decided to 'test' this Jeanne girl and he placed a knight on the throne while he hid in the crowd. Jeanne entered the throne room and walked straight up to the real prince and said God led her to him. A miracle?"

"It seems that way," I admitted.

The duke shook his head sadly. "I know people who were there at that first meeting. The story is a fairy tale believed by fools. Charles was on his throne."

"She could hardly miss him," the knight roared. "Charles is a skinny little knock-kneed feller with one blue eye and one brown! No miracle there. But tell Brother John about the soldier on guard at Chinon."

The duke looked at me with his bloodshot eyes and said, "Explain this, master monk. As Jeanne rode into Chinon Castle a common soldier on guard at the gate shouted rude things at her. Jeanne turned to him and said, 'My friend, you should not have such evil thoughts. If only you knew how near you are to death.' Two hours later the soldier fell in the River Vienne and drowned."

"God will punish the wicked," I said. It seemed everyone round the table heard me and laughed.

"I think he believes it," someone cried. I turned red and buried my face in a goblet of wine.

"The problem with Jeanne was that she thought God was on the side of the French! And at first he seemed to be," de Baudricourt went on. "Jeanne the Maid was sent to the town of Orleans. It had been under siege by the English for a few months. She thought she was going to fight. In fact she was sent with supplies for the townspeople. You've never been to Orleans?"

"This will be my first visit," I said.

The duke leaned forward and a gust of beef and wine-smelling breath swept over me. "Orleans is on the north bank of the River Loire, you know. Jeanne's escort took her to the south bank to avoid the English troops. There was a gale blowing – and it was blowing directly against Jeanne and her supply wagons. There was no way the ferries could cross the river in that sort of storm. Jeanne was impatient. She didn't want to wait. So what happened? The wind stopped suddenly, then it started up again minutes later in the other direction! It blew them easily across the river."

"Lucky," one of the knights sneered.

"Or a miracle," the duke said. He went on, "Now

Jeanne wanted a good fight. Her voices had told her to drive the English out of France. She said she would be wounded in battle but that didn't matter. At last she got her chance. She was part of a raid on the English stronghold – Les Augustins – and of course you can't attack a fortress without a struggle."

"But Jeanne did it?" I asked eagerly.

"Jeanne's men were beaten back time and again," said the duke harshly. "The English are good fighters. At last the French retreated . . . and the English did a stupid thing. They left the safety of the fortress and chased after Jeanne's army. The French turned – the fight was on level ground now – and as darkness fell the English were massacred."

"Some say the way the English threw away their advantage was a miracle," the knight nodded.

"The next day Jeanne was wounded taking another English fortress . . . just as she said she would be." Robert de Baudricourt sighed. "She recovered from the arrow in the neck – it might have been better if she hadn't."

"But she was driving the English back," I said.

"She was," the duke agreed. "And she saw her dream of having the prince crowned as Charles VII in Reims. They marched through enemy territory all the way to Reims Cathedral. Enemy towns surrendered to Charles and the Maid. I was there when they placed the crown on Charles's funny little head. Jeanne stood close to him. I had to admit the impossible had happened. Prince Charles was King Charles VII and the English were on the run."

"And then?" I asked.

"And then the miracles dried up. Charles let her try to take Paris . . . but his heart wasn't in it. Jeanne wanted to fight – King Charles always preferred talking and making deals. When she reached Paris the odds were against her – and God wasn't with her that day." The noisy group of eaters at the table became strangely quiet as their duke described Jeanne's final defeat.

"The people of Paris were ready for Jeanne and her soldiers. The walls of the city were strong and tall. Their crossbow bolts rained down. Jeanne was wounded in the leg and taken from the battlefield. Her men failed to take the

city and Charles ordered her to give up the attempt."

"She failed," the knight put in. "For the first time she'd failed. You have to understand, young monk, war is like a tide. When it flows your way you sweep everything before you. But when that tide turns you are washed away like a grain of sand."

"Did they capture her then?" I asked.

"No. That wasn't until the following Easter, 1430," de Baudricourt explained. "She went on a raid against a band of England's allies from Burgundy. She left Crépy in Valois with two hundred men. They weren't strong enough. They were driven back to Crépy. As Jeanne retreated towards the castle the drawbridge was raised. Jeanne was shut out. It could be that she was betrayed. The Burgundian soldiers dragged her from her horse. She was a prisoner. They held her to ransom. No one came to her rescue."

"Charles?" I said. "What about Charles – the man she made king?"

"He didn't try to rescue her. He didn't offer a ransom to get her back. She was no more use to him. The English paid for her and took her to Rouen for trial."

"The king betrayed her!" I cried.

De Baudricourt turned his small, hard eyes on me. "Don't look to blame the king. Look to your own friends, master monk. It was the Church who tried her as a witch. It was your precious God who sent her into battle, then deserted her."

There was silence in the Great Hall. Even the dogs stopped crunching on their bones. At last I said, "And do you believe she is still alive?"

The duke reached forward and snatched a chicken leg from the table. "Will that chicken ever live again?" he asked. "No. That's one miracle I'll never believe."

"Then who is in Orleans?"

"You may find out when you get there," he said.

5

The next day's journey was gloomier than the one through the forest. The sky was covered with pearl-grey cloud. The road was lonely and the villages we passed through were deserted. No food for passing travellers. We rested beside a roofless and ruined cottage.

"I've got plenty to eat," Ellie said. "Took it from Duke Robert's table while you were talking . . . and, before you say anything, it's not stealing. We were his guests. I just kept some for later, that's all. Have some beef," she offered.

"Ellie, monks don't eat the meat of animals with four legs," I told her.

She thought about this for a moment. "Don't worry, this was from a three-legged bull," she said seriously. "I saw it hopping around in the field outside the castle."

I had to laugh. I said a quick prayer for God to forgive me then ate the beef with some bread. "Should I see if there's still fresh water?" I asked, pointing to the well in the centre of the village.

"Don't be stupid, Johnny," Ellie sighed. "Don't you know why this village is deserted?"

"The wars, I suppose."

"More likely the plague," she said. "I wouldn't drink that water. Some people think the disease came from poisoned water."

"And some people said it was an angel of death who rapped at your door with a spear."

"Do you believe that?" she asked.

I had believed it. Everything in the monastery had seemed so clear and simple. Here, in the outside world, you had to rely on your faith.

I remembered some of the letters I'd had to copy as writing practice. One was from an Italian poet called Petrarch to his brother who was a monk. The brother had been the only one of thirty-five brothers to survive when the plague came to their monastery. I looked around the deserted village and remembered the letter. I recited it for Ellie. "My brother, my brother, alas, what shall I say? Where shall I turn? On all sides is sorrow, everywhere is fear. I wish that I had never been born, or at least had died before these times. Who has ever seen houses so empty? Cities are deserted, the fields are too small to hold the dead, and a fearful and universal loneliness covers the whole earth."

Ellie looked around the ghost village. "I wish I could read and write," she said softly. "But women never learn to read, do they?"

"Not usually," I said.

"Can we go now?" she asked. "I don't like this place. Ninety years since the plague and the people still haven't come back. Can't blame them."

We continued on our way, still feeling the chill of death. Ellie finished gnawing on a swan's wingbone and then thrust it into my bag. "There you are," she said. "Saint whatsit's finger. The old abbot will never know," she grinned and her cheerful spirits began to return.

6

The monastery near Orleans was larger than mine back in Metz. "I have brought letters and a gift for your abbot," I told the brother at the gate.

"Come in, come in," he said. "You look as if you've walked a long way," he said frowning down on my worn sandals and dusty feet.

"From Metz," I said.

"Then we'd better make sure you have new sandals before you return," he said.

"Can I have a pair too?" Ellie put in.

The brother raised his eyebrows, "But of course," he said.

"Girls aren't allowed in a monastery," I said quickly.

"Oh, that rule doesn't apply here. Your girlfriend is welcome," he said, waving his hand towards the entrance.

"She's not my . . . she's my guide," I said, embarrassed and confused.

"Whatever," the brother shrugged. "Not all monasteries are as strict as yours. Monks live here with their wives and their children," he explained.

Back at Metz, Brother Michael had said that such places existed. I hadn't believed him.

Ellie jumped forward before I could argue any more. "I'll come and see what the abbot has to say," she said.

"Have you never met a real live abbot before?" the gatekeeper asked happily as he led the way into the monastery.

"No. Nor a real dead one," Ellie laughed with the man. I scowled and prayed that God's angels would take me up on a cloud – or even devils take me to hell – anything would be better than this.

Abbot Richard was red-faced and sly-eyed. He read the letters quickly while Ellie and I sat and drank watered wine and ate chicken. He scarcely glanced at St Anthony's armbone. Maybe he'd seen such fakes before, I thought uncomfortably. I wondered if there were any true miracles left in the world. "So you come from Metz, eh?" he smiled. "Which way did you come?"

"Through Domremy," I told him.

"Ah, the Maid's village," he nodded.

"You knew her?" I asked.

"Better than any. I was her personal priest before the English captured her and put her on trial."

"And you've heard

that she's returned?" I said.

He folded his hands across his fat stomach and sat back in his chair. "I met her yesterday," he said.

"And is it really Jeanne the Maid?" I asked.

"Did you ever hear how I met her?" he asked suddenly.

"No."

"I was with the English, you know."

"The enemy?"

"They are all very much the same. Simple soldiers fighting a pointless, endless war. The English believed Jeanne the Maid was a devil. I was preaching in Paris at the time. The English sent me to exorcize this Maid who'd been giving them so much trouble. I walked in to the French camp outside Troyes in 1429 and she came to meet me. I sprinkled holy water on her in the shape of a cross. The dear girl laughed! 'Don't worry,' she said. 'I won't fly away. I'm not a devil or a witch.' And, do you know, I believed her. From that moment I was her most devoted follower . . . until her capture, that is."

"Do you believe in her miracles?" Ellie put in.

The abbot spread his hands wide and his gold rings sparkled in the dusty rays of the sun. "There were a lot of silly stories told about her. They said she flew from the window of her prison after she was captured. The truth is she saw the English coming to take her to trial. She said she'd rather die than fall into the hands of the English. So she jumped from her window – she fell and hurt herself quite badly. Whether she wanted to escape, or to kill herself, I don't know."

"Did you go to her trial?" I asked.

"Ah, no. Remember I had left the English to support Jeanne and the French. I would not have been welcome. But I know many of the witnesses who were there. It was the Church who tried her for sorcery, not the English. They questioned her for fourteen months and she was accused of wearing men's clothes – which, as you know, Brother John, is against God's laws. She also said she took her orders directly from God, not from the Church. That made the Church really angry. Jeanne insisted her voices were from God – the Church said they were from the Devil. She was very stubborn about that."

"Well, she would be stubborn if she thought she was right," Ellie said.

The abbot turned his gooseberry-green eyes on Ellie. "Would you be stubborn, girl?"

"Of course," she said.

"Even if they tortured you?" he said in a voice as harsh as a steel knife on granite stone.

"They didn't, did they?" I whispered.

"No. The Church did not want to be seen as cruel. They wanted to be seen as kind and forgiving. They were clever. They sent a priest to her cell at night. He told her about the death that waited for her. Burning at the stake. The next morning she was taken to the old cemetery at Saint-Ouen. The executioner stood on his cart, waiting to take her away to the flames. The dead lay all around her in their cold graves. Could you have stood that?" the abbot asked.

I shuddered. Ellie lifted her chin proudly. "Jeanne didn't give in," she said. "That's why they burned her. I wouldn't have given in if I'd been Jeanne."

Abbot Richard showed yellow teeth in a wide grin. "You are wrong. Jeanne did give in. She admitted she had lied about the voices. She admitted that she was a sinner. She admitted anything they wanted so long as they didn't burn her!"

I was confused. "I thought they did burn her," I frowned. "Robert de Baudricourt said they did . . . everyone knows they did."

The abbot looked pleased with himself. "Jeanne signed

her confession with a cross. They sentenced her to life imprisonment. They shaved her hair and handed her over to the English to lock her away. That shocked Jeanne. She thought she was going to be set free! So she put on her man's clothing again and said she would rather die than stay in prison."

"And that was when they burned her," Ellie said.

"Three days later they brought the cart to take her to the stake in the old market square in Rouen. She was dressed in a simple white dress and had to wear a paper hat with her crimes written on it. The stake was built extra high so all the crowd could see her suffering. Jeanne asked for a cross – a soldier made one from two twigs tied together. Then the executioner lit the fire. It was over quickly. They do say that when they gathered her ashes Jeanne's heart was untouched by the flames . . . but that's probably just another story."

"It's not as strange as the story of her coming back to life," I said. "Yet you believe that!"

He folded his hands across his stomach. "That wasn't strange. It was simple. The English didn't want to kill

Jeanne the Maid. They simply wanted her out of the way. So the story is that they made a deal with the Maid. If she would take part in a little conjuring trick then she could live. Jeanne was whisked out of prison the night before the execution – they put another witch on the stake in her place. Simple," he smiled. "See for yourself tomorrow. She is meeting the people of Orleans."

7

It was restful for me to be in the shelter of a monastery again. I went to the usual night-time services and prayed. The only thing that troubled me was Ellie's doubts about Abbot Richard's story.

"I don't like him," she said. "He's as slippery as a pig's tongue. He worked for the English and he worked for the French. Just so long as he was on the winning side."

"But his story about the English switching a witch for Jeanne is believable," I argued.

She looked at me with pity in those dark, sharp eyes. "That is the least believable thing of all," she said. "Jeanne would do almost anything to save her life – but she would never let another woman die for her. Never. Everyone makes up their own mind about Jeanne. I think Jeanne was mad to behave the way she did. Her mother thinks she's a child, the people of Orleans think she's a heroine. De Baudricourt thinks she was strong, Abbot Richard thinks she was weak. But no one ever accused her of being cruel. And to let someone die so that she could live . . . what is crueller than that?" she asked.

I had no answer. It troubled me.

The next day we stood in the crowds that packed the streets of Orleans. The crowd was in a holiday mood. Pie-sellers mingled with pickpockets and priests. Everyone had their own story to tell about Jeanne and the time when she saved Orleans from the English.

Soldiers began to push the crowds from the road. Ellie and I were crushed against the wooden walls of a house. Ellie pulled herself up till she was sitting on my shoulder. I struggled to see past a solid peasant in a leather jerkin. I could see a richly dressed man ride down the main street on a fine white horse. "That's Madame du Lys's son. That's Jeanne's brother Jacquemin," Ellie shouted over the noise of the cheering crowds.

The cries grew deafening as an open carriage came slowly into sight. The woman had her dark hair cut like a man's. She was dressed as a soldier – grey tunic and black leggings. The helmet shaded her face but I could make out straight, dark eyebrows over blank, cold eyes. She carried a white banner.

As she waved to the excited people they pressed forward to touch her and the carriage was almost forced to halt. Armed men pushed the people back and I was crushed in the crowd. Ellie slipped from my shoulder and in a few

minutes I lost her. When the people moved down the street to follow the carriage I saw her leaning against the wall of a house. She was strangely pale and quiet.

"Well?" I asked her.

"Well," she said. "It's time we went back to Domremy."

"I thought you were staying in the city," I said.

"I think I ought to go back one more time. Just to see Madame du Lys. Just to tell her that we've found her daughter."

Part Two

The Fact Files

1 THE PEOPLE FILE

Here are some true facts about the main characters in the story. What sort of people are they? Can you trust what they did or said?

Jeanne the Maid.

Name: *Jeannette Darc (or Tarc)*
– her family name in Domremy
Jeanne la Pucelle (Jeanne the Maid)
– the name she chose for herself
Joan of Arc – the name historians gave
her fifty years after her death
Saint Joan – the title given to her by
the Church 500 years after her death

Appearance: Below average height, black hair cut short, above the ears, so her helmet would fit. Strong and healthy. She is never mentioned as being beautiful so some historians take this as a sign that she must have been ugly!

Character: Jeanne seemed a perfectly ordinary girl until the age of thirteen – the age when she said she first saw and heard her visions. Then she became much more religious: she would stop playing in the fields and fall to her knees to pray; she would travel a long way to attend church regularly. She could also be very stubborn and would often persist when everyone else wanted to give up. She always argued that she was not doing what she wanted – she was doing what God wanted . . . and God wanted Charles to be crowned and the English driven out of France.

Problem: Jeanne went into battle with a banner, not a sword. She saw her job as encouraging the French to drive out the English.

King Charles VII

Name: *Charles the Dauphin*
– prince and heir to the throne
King Charles VII of France – after
his coronation in 1429
The so–called King of France –
that's what his English enemies
called him

Appearance: Clean shaven with
every scrap of hair tucked under his hat. Small narrow eyes,
close together, long nose with a bulge at the end drooping
over a thick, short top lip. Yet an enemy historian wrote that
Charles was "pale-faced, but handsome enough".

Character: Charles never liked fighting – he left that to his
generals. He was a good scholar and as religious as Jeanne.
He was also superstitious – he never walked on a floor or a
bridge unless it had been tested for safety; he avoided
strangers and large groups of people, maybe fearing
assassination. He was very crafty – he preferred getting what
he wanted through clever plots rather than fighting.

Problem: Jeanne had helped him to defeat the English and be
crowned at Reims. Did he desert her and let the enemy burn
her? Did he give her up when she was no more use to him?
Or did he try to make a deal with the English – "Let her live
and I promise she will never lead an army against you again"?

Abbot Richard
Name: *Full name unknown*

Appearance: Unknown. Dressed in the brown robes of a Franciscan friar.

Character: A very powerful and popular preacher. When he was in Paris, on the side of the English, he preached against gambling – he preached all day long for ten days in a row! Thousands flocked to hear him. The people were so upset by his harsh words that they made a huge bonfire of all their gaming boards, cards and dice . . . When he deserted to the French side they made new ones and started gambling again! He was treated with great respect by everyone because he had a fondness for protecting women with mystic powers – women who could see into the future or who, like Jeanne, claimed to speak to God. The English churchmen began to suspect that he was in partnership with the Devil himself and were starting to investigate him. That's when he changed sides and 'adopted' Jeanne. He later took a woman called Catherine into his care. Catherine claimed to speak to a "white lady dressed in gold". Jeanne proved Catherine was in fact a fake – "mad and a liar", she said. Abbot Richard and Jeanne fell out over this.

Problem: The abbot knew the Maid well, and could have identified the 'Jeanne' who appeared in Orleans. Would he lie and say it was Jeanne . . . even if he knew she was a fake? And why would he lie?

The du Lys Family
Names: *Jeanne the Maid*
Jacques, Jeanne's father,
died 1439
Zabillet (or Isabel), Jeanne's
mother

Jacquemin, Jean and Pierre,
Jeanne's three older brothers
Catherine, her sister, about
whom almost nothing is
known.
The family name was *Darc* but,
in honour of *Jeanne*, the king
gave them the title *Du Lys*.

Appearance: Short and dark-haired like Jeanne, except for
Madame du Lys who was tall.

Character: The men were very ambitious. Jacques, Jeanne's
father, was a little better off than the peasants in the village –
his house was made of stone, not wood, and his ancestors
had been nobles. He hated the idea of Jeanne dressing as a
soldier and going off to fight – until she became a success
and a favourite of the king. Suddenly he approved.
Jacquemin, Jean and Pierre were quick to join their sister
while she was winning. When towns poured gifts on Jeanne
her brothers received gifts too – money, horses and fine
clothes. Of course they were not around when she was tried
as a witch, but they were seriously affected.

Problem: When Jeanne died at the stake the family's days of
rich gifts were over – unless she could return from the dead.
Would they have taken part in a fraud? Would they lie to and
cheat the people of Orleans?

FACT FILES

2 THE TIME FILE

1337 English kings say they are also kings of France – the French disagree. The Hundred Years' War starts . . . and lasts for 116 years! The fighting is interrupted by . . .

1348 the Black Death – the plague – which reaches France and kills far more people than the wars against the English ever did. And in . . .

1395 there is a truce in the Hundred Years' War, until

1411 when King Charles VI goes mad. The French begin to fight among themselves for his throne. The English take the chance of starting the war again and in . . .

1415 win a great victory against the French at Agincourt. Meanwhile in . . .

1412 (or perhaps late in 1411) Jeanne is born in Domremy. The exact date is unknown because 'birthdays' weren't important to people like Jeanne and her family at that time. It could have been on 6 January. Then in . . .

1422 Charles VI dies – but has said Henry of England should have the French crown! His son, Charles VII, disagrees and restarts the war with the English. Back in Domremy . . .

1425 Jeanne, now about thirteen, begins to hear the voices of St Margaret, St Catherine and St Michael, then in . . .

1428 (May) Jeanne visits Robert de Baudricourt and asks him to support her journey to Prince Charles to save France. De Baudricourt refuses. Shortly afterwards in . . .

1428 (early summer) a young man says Jeanne promised to marry him, then changed her mind. He takes her to court. Jeanne defends herself and wins the case. Suddenly . . .

1428 (July) Jeanne's village is attacked by supporters of the English king. The people are forced to flee to a nearby town. So . . .

1428 (autumn) Jeanne visits de Baudricourt a second time. This time he agrees to support her. She leaves to meet Prince Charles.

1429 (Easter) Jeanne rides 400 miles through enemy territory to meet Charles.

1429 (May) Jeanne and the French drive the English away from Orleans. Her first great victory. Then in . . .

1429 (July) Charles is crowned at Reims – Jeanne's second great success. But . . .

1430 Jeanne's last battle. She is captured and sold to the English. After a trial . . .

1431 (May 30) Jeanne is burned at the stake as a witch. Or was she? Because in . . .

1436 (July) 'Jeanne the Maid' appears miraculously in Orleans! The Maid's brother visits the king and asks for money. The king and the people of Orleans come up with just a few pounds. But later, in . . .

1439 (summer) 'Jeanne the Maid' appears again. This time she is honoured with a huge feast . . . and hundreds of pounds of money. Then she mysteriously disappears again.

1452 Jeanne's trial is held again – without her, of course. This time she is found not guilty!

Did you know . . . King Charles VI's sister, Isabella, was married to England's King Richard II in 1396. This was meant to bring peace between the two countries. Isabella's feelings didn't matter. After all, she was just seven years old at the time. Richard was murdered three years later. Isabella was a widow at the age of ten!

3 THE LIFESTYLE FILE

The characters of John the monk and Ellie the farm labourer are fictional, but believable. What sort of lives would they have lead?

A day in the life of a medieval monk

2:00 a.m. *Matins.* First service of the day. I was deep asleep when the bell rang. We sleep in our robes. All I have to do is slip on my sandals and walk down the dark stone stairway to the church. Wilfred trips me and I stumble into the back of fat Brother Michael. The monk picks me up with one hand and uses the other to beat me with his cane. It's hard to sit through two hours of prayer with lashes burning your back and a draught freezing your feet. They say an old English king called Cnut gave the monks at one monastery a gift to keep them warm – twelve polar bear skins to make winter boots! I wonder what a polar bear looks like.

6:00 a.m. *Prime.* I was trying to sleep lying on my face because my back hurt so much. I finally fell asleep as the bell rang for the next service, Prime. I'm so tired. We wash in the trough in the cloisters. There's ice on the top this morning. I splash it on my face, but the cold water doesn't wake me. Saint Benedict said the first rule is to praise God at least eight times a day. I wonder if God ever needs to sleep.

7:00 a.m. *Breakfast.* Silence while we're eating, of course. Wilfred whispers something in my ear, I say "What was that?" and I'm punished with three days on bread and water. I think that's probably better than the porridge I have to eat now. The rules are strict; the abbot says, "No monk should use the tablecloth to wipe his nose or clean his teeth!" No one will tell me why. I'll just have to sniff.

8:00 a.m. A quick wash in the lavatorium, then off to the daily meeting in the chapter house. The abbot says the monastery is wasting too much money on food. It isn't spent at our meal table I can tell you! We look to the guest-master; we know he has been spending too much money entertaining guests. We finish with prayers for the dead. If the dead are warm and cosy in heaven, why do we need to pray for them?

9:00 a.m. *Terce.* Another service, then off to work. The second of Benedict's rules is work. Today I had to practise writing in the scriptorium. Wilfred gets to work in the kitchens. It's warm there and he can take all the food he wants – so long as no one catches him! Benedict's third rule is about controlling yourself. I hope Benedict is up in heaven watching Wilfred stuffing himself.

11:00 a.m. *High Mass.* The big service of the day. Then off to the fields to dig until my back breaks. I look at the calves hungrily. I hear that some monks eat the meat of beasts. We'll kill our calves soon, then use the skin from their bellies to make the vellum that we write on. If we can use their skin why can't we eat their meat? I ask Brother Michael.

He beats me again. I eat bread and water for my midday meal and wonder what beef tastes like. I'm hungry and feel weak. Brother Michael tells me of an English monk who was asked what he ate. The monk replied, "Yesterday I had peas and herbs – today, herbs and peas. Tomorrow I shall eat peas with my herbs – the day after, herbs with my peas." I'm sure Brother Michael didn't get fat eating peas or herbs.

3:00 p.m. *Nones.* After the service there are three more hours of lessons. I have to copy out the ten main sins of monks. I think I commit most of the sins every day. A sinful monk:

1. Thinks too much of his own comfort
2. Is tempted by rich food
3. Makes a noise in the cloister
4. Argues with brother monks
5. Is disorderly in church
6. Is careless
7. Disobeys senior monks
8. Is lazy as an old monk
9. Wants his own way
10. Thinks of the world outside.

How many of these sins would you have committed?

–48–

6:00 p.m. *Vespers*. I'm hungry already. The abbot tells the story of the monk Odo. The rule in his monastery was that every crumb had to be picked up after a meal and eaten so there was no waste. Odo prayed so hard he forgot to pick up the crumbs. As the other monks left the dining room he scrambled after them, gathering crumbs as he went. He apologised to the abbot. "What for?" the abbot asked. "For not eating my crumbs," Odo replied. He opened his hand to show the abbot the crumbs . . . but his hand was full of pearls! A miraculous reward for a very holy man? Personally I'd rather have the crumbs.

7:00 p.m. *Compline*. The last service of the day, then a quick wash and bed. I've heard that Carthusian monks have their own sleeping cells. I wish we had. I share with twelve others. Fat Brother Michael snores and Wilfred torments me. I'll try to get a few hours' sleep before the day starts again. My parents placed me in this monastery because they said it would be a better life than being peasant workers like them. I'm not so sure. I often commit sin ten and think of the world outside. I think I'd quite like to be a peasant.

Did you know . . . In the 1390s a craftsman in Wurtzburg, Germany, made the first alarm clock. It was meant for use in monasteries where the monks had to pray at regular hours.

Someone else's life always seems more attractive than your own. If Ellie could have written, how would she have described her life?

A year in the life of a medieval peasant

January: The fields are wet and muddy. My feet are so wet I can't even feel them. The corn we gathered in the summer is stale now and the meat has been salted to stop it rotting. We add a few herbs to take the disgusting taste away. If we were rich we'd be able to afford spices. They say the kitchens up at the castle use something called 'sugar' to flavour their sweet foods. It's so precious they keep it locked away. I don't suppose I'll ever get to taste sugar.

February: Food is getting short now. We're eating thinner stews. But we're not the only ones to go hungry. Bands of soldiers are roaming the country looking for food. We try to hide it and tell them we have nothing, but it's hard to lie with a sword at your throat. Sometimes we try to hide ourselves as well. The villagers of Domremy know of an island in the middle of the river where we're usually safe. A bell rings to signal that raiders are on the way. Even the cows know what the bell means. They head for the island as soon as they hear it. If we're lucky the raiders will miss the food we've buried. If we're not, they'll go off hungry, but burn our homes.

March: This month we plough. Oxen do the pulling but we take turns following the plough. The wind is still bitter.

April: Things are starting to grow again. The sheep have lambs and the seeds are sown in the fields. My job is building a scarecrow to keep the birds from eating the seeds. I've given him a crossbow. Perhaps he'll scare the soldiers away.

May: Everyone's in a mood to celebrate. We put a maypole in the field and dance and feast. Of course some of the religious ones say we should be praying instead. Then it's back to work again.

June: It's time to shear the sheep to keep them cool over the summer. The sheep are luckier than the humans, but trying to keep a sheep still is hard work.

July: It's so hot and dusty that I spend half my time running back to the village to fetch water and ale for the men as they cut the hay. My neck is burned and sore from the sun. Fine ladies have white skin. Mine is brown as the dust.

August: My body is covered in bee stings. I was told to beat the iron drum that brings the bees back to their hives, but they swarmed on me instead. My father just laughed. Everyone is busy in the fields cutting the corn.

September: It's time to pull the vegetables from the ground and pick fruit from the trees. The men are threshing the corn, beating it with wooden flails to separate the grain from the dry stalks.

October: The forest leaves are falling now. We go into the woods to gather branches and logs to keep us warm through the winter. Cutting and dragging and stacking from morning till night. Then there are the grapes to be crushed with our feet to make wine.

November: This is the time for ploughing and sowing the winter wheat and the pig has to be slaughtered and salted for winter food. The rich can afford beef. We dry some pig-meat in the smoke over the fire. The rest we pack into barrels of salt. We'll taste nothing but that smoke and salt for the next six months.

December: The days are short. Now is the time to spin the wool from the sheep we sheared in June. At least we can do that in front of the fire. We weave it till our fingers bleed. Then we make new clothes. And that's the end of another year. If I were a boy I'd be a monk – they seem to have an easy life.

Farmyard fun

Of course the peasants had some things to look forward to. Even a poor village held a Christmas feast. Then there were country sports and games. While the rich went hunting, the poor found simpler pleasures like this:

A game in which young men propel a huge ball, not by throwing it into the air but by striking and rolling it along the ground, and not with their hands but with their feet. A disgusting game, more common, offensive and worthless than any other game.

Do we still play this game today? Yes. We call it soccer (or football). Which of these modern games were played (in a simple form) in medieval times?

Hockey	True/false?
Ice skating	True/false?
Throwing quoits	True/false?
Bowling	True/false?
Archery	True/false?
Blind man's buff	True/false?
Tennis	True/false?
Golf	True/false?

Answer: All were played.

Ice skates were made from cattle bones and used on frozen ponds.

Archery was compulsory in Britain – in 1467 a Scottish king even banned football because it got in the way of archery practice. It was this practice that helped the English archers do so well in the Hundred Years' War.

Blind man's buff was supposed to have been invented after a French knight called Colin, who was blinded in battle, but continued fighting by lashing out with his weapons.

Tennis balls were not made of soft rubber but solid wood. People struck by tennis balls sometimes died.
Golf became popular in Scotland and Holland in the fifteenth century.

Of course monks were not supposed to have fun . . . but the young ones often did. A medieval manuscript describes a group of young monks dropping hot candle wax on to the bald heads of old monks who fell asleep in church.

Villainous villagers

In England someone who lived in a village was called a villein. But some villeins were such rough and criminal types that 'villein' came to mean 'villain'! Peasants were important in medieval Europe. Some people appreciated them. Jacques de Vitry, a priest, wrote :

"They lead a wretched life – poor, suffering and beggarly. But without this race of people I truly do not know how the rest would survive."

But Jacques de Vitry was the odd one out. Most of the richer people hated peasants. One writer said: "The peasant's head is so hard that no ideas can get into it."

Another claimed: "Even the devil won't take a peasant. The smell is too bad."

And another said: "We should think of these peasants as a type of cattle."

Terrible towns

The towns seemed very attractive to the peasants. When they had more freedom, after the Black Death, many moved to the towns. Would you have liked to live in a medieval town?

Rubbish and slops were thrown out of windows into the streets which swarmed with rats and flies – wild birds and pet pigs or dogs might fight over it. Horse, pig and dog droppings were everywhere.

A night guard of ordinary citizens patrolled the streets with torches. There were no street lights. Anyone out after 9p.m. without good reason could be arrested and locked away.

In some towns, public toilets were built over ditches which led into the river. This, of course, polluted the drinking water. Criminals at medieval Strasbourg in Germany were ducked in the river – at the point where the sewers ran into it!

Towns were also violent places in which to live. There was as much crime in medieval times as at any time in history. Everyone was out to earn money — honestly or dishonestly.

Did you know . . . King Louis IX of France (1226-70) took an early morning walk. Suddenly someone emptied something out of the window and soaked his cloak. It was a young man emptying a chamber pot he had used as a toilet during the night. The king ran into the house and found it was a student who had tipped the mess over him. The student said he had got up early to study. The king was impressed and offered to pay for the student's education. (Of course Louis IX was a saint. Others might not have been so forgiving.)

Crime and punishment

Name: *Maurice the Miller*
Crime: Deception
What he did: Everyone must take their corn to the miller for grinding into flour. The miller takes a share of the flour as his payment. Like most millers, Maurice fills half the farmer's sack with sand or plaster and only half with flour. He keeps the rest of the flour for himself.
Punishment: A fine

Name: *Dunois the Draper*
Crime: Fraud
What he did: Gives short measures of cloth and tells customers that his cheap cloth is finest quality, dyed with the best dyes that will last a lifetime. The customer discovers that the colour runs out of it the first time it is washed.
Punishment: Using false weights and measures was punished by the ducking stool. Butchers who sold horsemeat instead of beef or bakers who put stones in bread were also punished by ducking. A cheating brewer would be made to drink huge quantities of his own beer and then have the rest poured over him.

Name: *Francois the Peasant*
Crime: Stealing sixteen eggs
What he did: His family was starving so he crept into a monastery henhouse and took the eggs. He was caught and taken to the abbot
Punishment: The abbot insisted that the peasant should be hanged.

Name: *Nell the Nag*
Crime: Shouting at her husband in public
What she did: Nell lost her temper with her husband. Instead of keeping the quarrel in the house she swore at him in the street.
Punishment: The woman might have been forced to walk through the streets wearing an iron mask to clamp her tongue still. A man who failed to control his wife would suffer all kinds of ridicule and be jeered at for being bossed by his wife.

Name: *Bertrand the Bully*
Crime: Beating his wife
What he did: When nagged by his wife he punched her and kicked her.
Punishment: None

Name: *Silly Sam*
Crime: Keeping a tame hawk he found
What he did: Anyone finding a hawk had to return it to the lord who owned it . . . or else!
Punishment: The hawk was fed 170 grams of flesh cut from the man's chest.

Did you know . . . It wasn't only the lower classes who suffered crime and punishment. One of Jeanne the Maid's most loyal soldiers, Giles de Rais, was accused of murdering 150 children . . . and confessed. But he could have been falsely accused; his accusers wanted to get their hands on his wealth. He may have confessed because that was the only way his family would be allowed to keep his riches. He was executed by strangling and burning.

4 THE FOOD FILE

If you'd like an even more realistic idea of medieval life then you could try a taste of it — literally! Try making some of these genuine medieval recipes.

Mixtum

Monks who did particularly hard work, or young novices who needed energy, would eat 'Mixtum' before their dinner. This was a quarter litre of beer and 100 grams of dry bread. Try it – using grape juice instead of beer, of course!

Arbolettys

Jeanne and the du Lys family, being a bit better off than peasants, might have eaten this meal of eggs with cheese and herbs.

Ingredients:
56 grams butter
170 grams grated cheese
8 eggs – size 3
1 teaspoon parsley
quarter teaspoon sage
quarter litre of milk
quarter teaspoon ginger

Method:
Place the milk, butter and cheese in a saucepan and warm them gently, stirring with a wooden spoon. When they are mixed smoothly, add the eggs, parsley, sage and ginger. Stir the mixture until it sets. Serve it on hot buttered toast.

Arbolettys can also be eaten cold for a picnic or as a snack when you are out in the fields cutting corn!

Tasty treats

In the Middle Ages some people advised eating pork because it was the nearest thing to human flesh! (How did they know?) Which of the following were sometimes eaten by medieval people?

1. Vultures   True/false?
2. Chips   True/false?
3. Cucumber   True/false?
4. Fruit jelly   True/false?
5. Tomatoes   True/false?

6.   Whale meat   True/false?
7.   Starlings   True/false?
8.   Cakes   True/false?
9.   Cornflakes   True/false?
10. Porpoises   True/false?

Answers:
True: **1, 4, 6, 7, 8, 10**.
False: **2.** (they had no potatoes); **3.** (they had cucumbers but thought they were unhealthy to eat); **5.** (they had no tomatoes); **9.** (they had no maize).

The peasants were stuck with porridge, beans, turnips and black bread without even a vulture for their Sunday dinner! (Meanwhile King John of England (1199-1216) was ordering that his hawks should be fed on chicken and pork!) A lord could hunt deer over a peasant's land – the same deer could destroy a peasant's crop of wheat, but the peasant wasn't allowed to touch it. Killing a deer was as serious as killing a man. And the punishment was usually the same – death.

Sickly sausages

This story was told in medieval France by a priest who swore it was true:

Fit for a feast

If you were invited to one of Robert de Baudricourt's feasts would you know how to behave? Test yourself with these ten questions . . . but remember, if you make even one mistake you could disgrace yourself!

1. When you first sit at the table a bowl of scented water will be passed around. Should you . . .
a) drink it
b) wash your feet in it
c) wash your hands in it?

2. Trumpets sound and drums roll. Does this signal mean . . .
a) the first course of food is being served
b) everyone must take the person on their right-hand side and dance with them
c) an enemy is attacking – draw your sword?

3. What should you take with you to the feast . . .
a) fork
b) knife and spoon
c) plate?

4. What would you eat your food from . . .
a) a wooden bowl
b) a silver plate
c) a slab of bread?

5. How would you sprinkle salt on to your food . . .
a) take some on the tip of your knife
b) take a pinch between your fingers
c) gather some on your spoon?

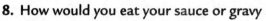

6. Would you keep your knife clean by wiping it . . .
a) on the tablecloth
b) on your breeches/skirt
c) on a piece of your bread?

7. What would you use to eat meat . . .
a) knife
b) spoon
c) fingers?

8. How would you eat your sauce or gravy . . .
a) dip your fingers in and lick them
b) use bread to mop it up
c) drink straight from the dish?

9. Who would get the *upper crust* of the slab of bread . . .
a) anyone who wanted it
b) the most important guest
c) the least important guest?

10. If someone asked you to "Splatt that pike (fish)," would you . . .
a) carve it and serve it
b) hit it with your spoon
c) pass it across the table?

Answers

1. *c)* Fingers had to be kept clean because everyone was handling the same food.
2. *a)* Trumpets and drums often announced each part of the meal in turn. A long meal could give you quite a headache!
3. *b)* Forks were not used until the 1600s. The most honoured guests were given a knife, a spoon and a napkin – everyone else was expected to bring their own spoon and

knife. Folding napkins for guests became an art form –
they were made into the shapes of birds and animals.

4. *c)* Separate plates were hardly ever used. Food was served
on large dishes, guests lifted their choice of food into a
dish lined with a slab of bread called a trencher. There
were frequent warnings about diving into a large dish of
food with your knife: "Watch your fingers don't get
mangled along with the joint of meat – it would be wise to
wear armoured gloves at some feasts!"

5. *a)* Dirty fingers dipped into the dish of salt would not be
welcomed by the other eaters at your table. Salt cellars
with which to sprinkle salt on to the food were not used
until long after the Middle Ages.

6. *c)* Clean knives were important – after all you couldn't
spear food with the knife, stick it in your mouth and then
put it back into the dish of food from which others would
be eating. Many people think the medieval people knew
nothing about hygiene and spreading germs. They did.

7. *c)* Fingers were washed at the end of each course.

8. *b)* Nowadays mopping up food with bread is thought
rather rude, but in medieval times everyone from a
peasant to a monarch did it.

9. *b)* The favourite part of the bread was the top (or upper)
crust and this went to the most important guest. Today
some people still talk about high-class people as 'the
upper crust'.

10. *a)* A medieval way of saying to split it. People had curious
expressions for serving each type of meat; you would
unjoint a bittern but mince a plover. You would display a
crane, but disfigure a peacock. You might tyre an egg but
unlace a rabbit, string an eel but tame a crab! They all
meant 'carve and serve' the food.

Manners makyth the man

By Jeanne's time, many books had been written about table manners in fine houses. But as peasants couldn't read these books they weren't expected to have any manners! Among the advice offered was . . .

✗ Do bow to the salt cellar on the lord's table when you enter the dining hall
✗ Do not butter bread with your thumbs
✗ Do not poke your fingers into egg yolks
✗ Do not spit across the table
✗ Do not scratch your head at the table
✗ Do not pick your nose at dinner
✗ Do not pick your teeth with your knife.

Did you know . . . Life in a monastery could be more luxurious than life outside. Some monks ignored the rules that said they should eat just once a day. They also ignored the rule against eating meat. In some medieval monasteries monks were allowed eight pints of beer a day, ate meat, wore jewels and gowns trimmed with fur. They were also given pocket money, and they used it to employ servants to do their work.

5 THE EVENTS FILE

The appearance of Jeanne the Maid to lead Charles VII's army was an important event in the medieval world — nothing was ever quite the same afterwards. But, as John and Ellie discovered on their journey, it wasn't the only event of importance in medieval Europe.

The Black Death

This killer started in the Gobi Desert in northern Asia. It spread to China where it wiped out *35 million* people. Then it was carried to Egypt by traders – and killed seven thousand people every day. Finally it reached Europe in 1347.

It became known as the Black Death.

No one in the medieval world knew what caused it, though they thought it might be bad air. In modern times scientists discovered that:

✗ fleas carried plague germs in their blood
✗ the fleas lived in the fur of rats and bit them
✗ the rats caught the plague and died
✗ the fleas looked for a new 'home', jumped on to humans and bit them
✗ the humans died.

Now everyone blames the rats and forgets that the plague came to Europe thanks to *humans*.

And it wasn't started accidentally. It was quite deliberate! This is how it happened . . .

Pass the plague

...... It all started over in Caffa on the coast of the Black Sea. Nice touch that — Black Sea — Black Death, geddit?......

You are a cheat and a liar!

Christian Dog!

·········Italian merchants were trading in Caffa

··And a little street fight turned into a war·····

POW!

Muslim villain!

·····The Muslims turned to Janibeg a local warlord for help...

We must drive the Christians back to Italy

First we will lay siege to Caffa and starve them out

····First I visited Janibeg's army and gave them a gift of the plague...

Why couldn't death visit the Christians?

So in 1347 the Black Death reached Genoa in Italy. By 1348 it had spread through France and Spain and had reached Britain and Germany by 1349. One person in every three died . . . painfully.

The Purple Death

It's called the Black Death, though Purple Death would be more accurate. Here are the symptoms . . .

- headache
- sickness
- aching joints
- painful swelling in the groins, the armpits or the neck – these are called 'buboes' and that's where the plague's other name, Bubonic Plague, comes from
- high temperature and shivering
- fast pulse rate
- fast breathing
- exhausted feeling
- the swellings grow to the size of a chicken's egg
- the victim's lungs fail to give the oxygen needed to keep the blood red, the victim turns purple . . . and then dies.

Because doctors had no cures medieval people tried all sorts of superstitious remedies:

Beating the Black Death

Running away was the answer for many people. While they were away their homes were robbed and their livelihood ruined of course. An English poet of the time, Geoffrey Chaucer, wrote a clever poem about Black Death runaways. It was published about twenty years before Jeanne the Maid was born. Called 'The Pardoner's Tale', it appeared in a collection of rhyming stories called **The Canterbury Tales.** *Here's a modern version. . .*

Death under the tree

Three men meet in a tavern and drink their ale. Let's call the men Tom, Dick and Harry. News comes to the inn of yet another old friend dead from plague. The three decide that they will have to flee the town and live deep in the forest till the plague has gone.

In fear and panic they run for miles, until they reach a lonely wood – no food, no drink, no money in their purses.

"This Black Death's an evil thing," Tom says.

"It is!" his friends agree.

"If I meet up with this chap Death . . . I'll kill him!" Harry boasts.

And at that moment, through the trees, a shadowy figure wanders by. A faceless figure in a hooded cloak. He looks like Death himself. With a voice as harsh as grating bones the figure whispers, "You will find Death underneath that tree."

The men laugh nervously. They start to dig and come across a box. Tom takes his knife and forces up the lid. But, as he lifts the knife to strike at Death, he stops – he blinks – he drops the knife. The box is full of gold.

The happy men decide to celebrate. "Go to the nearest town and buy us wine and bread," Harry orders Dick.

Grumbling, Dick goes off to find some plague-free town.

Then Tom and Harry gloat about their gold. "We're rich!" Harry sighs happily.

"Ah, yes, but we'll be richer still if we take old Dick's gold.

We'll share it out between us two!"

"We can't do that! He'll kill us if we take his gold," Harry mumbled.

"He can't kill us," Tom says with gold glints in his eyes. "Not if we kill the fat fool first!"

And that's what they decide. They lie in wait for Dick with daggers drawn.

"Hi, lads! I'm back!" their old friend cries. "I've brought the wine . . . you don't need knives to sup your wine, so put them down . . . hey . . . what you at!" he cries. And then he cries no more.

"Here, pass the wine," says Tom, trembling, and he gulps it down.

"He was our friend," the heartless Harry nods, and takes a deep, deep drink.

"The wine tastes off," Tom says, clutching at his burning throat. He falls face down upon the grass beneath the tree.

"You're right!" his blood-soaked friend gasps, "the fiend has poisoned this here wine so he could rob us of our gold!"

he says before he falls, dead, by the other two. And from the shadows of the trees a grey-cloaked figure wanders out. The faceless form just stretches out a bony hand and gathers up the gold. A grinning skull, as cold as Death himself, looks down and says, "I warned the fools that Death lay underneath that tree."

After the Black Death

But what effect did the Black Death have on Jeanne the Maid's life eighty years later?

Before the Black Death . . .   *After the Black Death . . .*

Peasant workers were slaves to the landowners. They had to stay on the farms and work for tiny rewards.

Peasant workers were in short supply. Landowners had to pay them double wages or they would move to the towns.

Landowners never dirtied their hands with work themselves.

Landowners saved money by doing some of the farm work themselves.

Landowners were often given noble titles – but a family with a title was not allowed to work on the land.

Some landowners, like the Darc family, gave up their titles so they could be working farmers.

The plague also had an effect on the Hundred Years' War . . .

Before the Black Death . . .

Peasant workers were given land. In return they had to fight for the landowner for little or no money.

Peasants fought for their king and their own country.

Because peasant soldiers were cheap a king could fight with large armies. The largest army of the Hundred Years' War was Edward III's in 1347 – a year before the Black Death.

After the Black Death . . .

Peasants were needed on the land. If a landowner wanted an army he had to pay professional soldiers.

Soldiers fought for any country that would pay them.

Large armies cost money. Taxes were hard to collect after the Black Death. Now battles were fought when leaders could afford to pay an army. The richest leader often had the largest army.

The Hundred Years' War

The plague returned in 1361, 1369, 1374, 1390 and 1400 and the war dragged on. There were very few big battles. It was mainly small armies capturing towns or raiding the enemy's farms, crops and animals. Did you know . . .

1.   The war didn't stop the armies having some sport. In 1337 Edward III took a large pack of hounds with him to France so he could go hunting when he wasn't fighting.

2.   In 1346 the French lost the first great battle of the Hundred Years' War at Crécy in northern France, when 38,000 French were beaten by 18,000 English and a heavy shower of rain! The English kept their longbows dry while the French crossbows were soaked and useless. Then the French knights tried to charge across a stream to attack the English, but the rain had turned it into a swamp. The English archers sent hundreds crashing down into the mud. Most of the French footsoldiers never got  near the battle. One of the few knights to reach the English was the King of Bohemia . . . and he was blind! Not surprisingly he was killed. (Don't feel too sorry for him. The king had paid a doctor to cure his blindness. When the doctor failed, the king had him sewn up in a sack and thrown in the River Oder to drown.)

3.   In the second great battle, at Poitiers in 1356, the French got it wrong again. France's King John told his knights to get off their horses to fight – the way the English had done at Crécy. But the English had been defending at Crécy. It's harder charging to attack with heavy armour on. England's Edward, the Black Prince, won and managed to capture the French king.

4. King John was taken to London and the English asked for a huge ransom before they would set him free. John's son said it was too much and refused to pay to have his father released. John lived in London while one-third of his ransom was scraped together and he was treated more as a guest than a prisoner. He died in London in 1360.

5. Many towns suffered sieges. The enemy armies surrounded them and tried to stop food supplies getting in. When the townspeople began to starve they would give up. But some armies became impatient. They tried destroying town walls by digging tunnels underneath them, then making the tunnels collapse. Towns needed a way of testing whether their walls were being 'mined' like this. The defenders placed bowls of water along the top of the walls. If the surface of the water trembled then the walls were being mined.

6. Henry V of England started a new attack on the French in 1415. This time he took cannon with him to help destroy the town walls. The cannon had nicknames such as: The London, The Messenger and The King's Daughter! The guns were almost four metres long but they

didn't fire their 200-kilogram shots very far. They had to be taken quite close to the town's walls to do any damage. As a result the defenders had a good chance of killing the gunners. And if the defenders didn't kill you then you could easily kill yourself . . . gunpowder was mixed on the battlefield and could easily explode and kill you as you tried to load or fire the gun.

7. In 1415 Henry's army of 6,000 English defeated 25,000 French at the Battle of Agincourt. Again, it was the power of the English archers that cut down the French knights – English longbowmen fired up to twenty arrows a minute. The French threatened they would cut off three fingers of the right hand of any English archers that they captured so they could never fire a bow again. The English archers were paid sixpence a day. The English were just as cruel – they were afraid their French prisoners would start fighting again, so they killed most of them in cold blood.

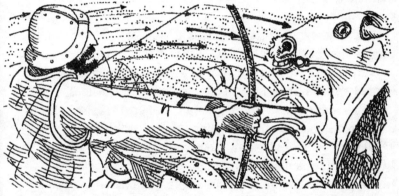

8. A peace was agreed in 1396 and the Hundred Years' War could have ended then. But Charles VI (Charles VII's father) started having attacks of madness. It began when he was riding with some guards and was frightened by an accidental blow to his helmet from a lance. He drew his sword and lashed out wildly. He killed four of his own men before he was disarmed and calmed down. In 1405 he suffered more serious mental problems when he refused to bathe or change his clothes for five months. Charles VI even declared that his crown should go to the English king when he died and not to Prince Charles. This was just the excuse the English wanted to return to the war. If it hadn't been for Charles VI's madness there would have been no problems for Charles VII . . . and there would have been no Jeanne the Maid.

9. One of France's problems was that it was not united. Some regions of France even joined forces with the English. Burgundy was a particularly difficult enemy and it was the forces of Burgundy that captured Jeanne and sold her to the English. However, Philip of Burgundy eventually gave up fighting because it was costing him too much money!

10. Charles VII went on to defeat the English and achieve Jeanne the Maid's dream. The Hundred Years' War ended in 1456 with victory for the French – twenty-five years after Jeanne's trial.

Did you know . . . fighting was a way of life for many noble Frenchmen in the fourteenth and fifteenth centuries. It was also a way of death. Arguments were often settled by a duel or single combat. The most curious case was that of a knight called Macaire. He was accused of killing another knight, Montdidier. He might have got away with it if Montdidier's dog, Dragon, had not kept attacking him. King Charles V ordered Macaire to fight in single combat with Dragon the dog! Macaire was armed with a thick pole but Dragon pinned him to the ground. Macaire begged for mercy, confessed to the murder and was hanged. Had he been 'hounded' to death?

What was the effect of the Hundred Years' War on Jeanne as she grew up? Apart from being attacked by raiding bands of soldiers, Jeanne was in the middle of the war from her earliest childhood . . . literally! Domremy village was split into two halves by a stream. Jeanne's half supported the French, the other half supported the English. Children would often cross the stream to throw stones – or just insults – at the children on the other side.

6 THE FAITH FILE

···

Today we know that witches don't exist except in stories. Did medieval people really believe that Jeanne was evil and sent by the Devil? Would the Church really burn someone who disobeyed it? Or did the English just use that as an excuse to get rid of a troublesome enemy? Look at the facts . . .

Witch ways

1. Another of Abbott Richard's mystic women followers was called Pieronne. She was captured at the same time as Jeanne and questioned by the Church. Pieronne spoke up for Jeanne. That was her first mistake. Her second mistake was to say that she too had chatted to God "as one friend does to another". The last time she saw God, she said, he'd been wearing a long white robe over a red tunic. She refused to change her story so she was burned in Paris on 3 September 1430.

2. Everyone in Jeanne's France would remember the case of King Philip the Fair of France. In 1307 he arrested a group of monks who had turned themselves into an army to fight in the Crusades. They called themselves the Templars. Philip accused the Templars of witchcraft; every Templar was imprisoned and forced to confess to witchcraft – or be tortured to death. In 1314 their leader, the Grand Master, was sent to the stake to be burned. Pope Clement agreed to the execution. As the fire curled upwards the Grand Master cried to Philip: "I shall meet you and Clement by God's judgement seat within a year. You and your descendants, for thirteen generations, will be cursed!" Pope Clement died within a month . . . King Philip died within seven months, though he was a healthy 46 year-old.

3. In 1374 Pope Gregory XI ordered the French Church to seek out and burn witches. A case in Paris in 1390 is a very good example. A woman hired a witch to cast spells to bring her lover back. Both the witch and the woman who hired her were burned at the stake.

4. Charles VI was never accused of witchcraft although he employed an astrologer called Thomas of Pisano. Apart from reading the king's fortune, Thomas also made wax images of the English and cast spells to destroy them. If you were a king you could get away with this sort of black magic.

5. Two monks tried to accuse King Charles's most powerful friend of witchcraft. They said the Duke of Orleans had used black magic to make Charles VI mad. Instead of trying the Duke, it was the monks who were tortured! They admitted they were liars and witches. They were executed. Accusing powerful people of witchcraft was a dangerous game.

Between the fourteenth and seventeenth centuries about half a million people (mainly women) died as witches in Europe – burned, hanged or drowned.

A sad superstition

Medieval people had some superstitions that we'd find strange today.

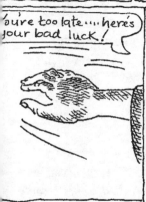

Silly spells

Everyone believed in magic — but no one believed that people who practised it should be burned as a witch! Ordinary people would try simple things to make life more comfortable.

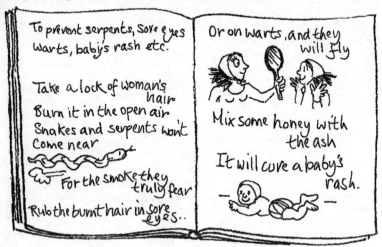

To prevent serpents, sore eyes
warts, baby's rash etc.

Take a lock of woman's hair
Burn it in the open air
Snakes and serpents won't
come near

For the smoke they truly fear

Rub the burnt hair in sore eyes..

Or on warts, and they will fly

Mix some honey with the ash
It will cure a baby's rash.

Jeanne wasn't accused of that sort of witchcraft — though the common English soldiers told tales of her magical powers. Her trial was to test if her 'angel voices' came from God or the Devil.

Did you know . . . The great dream of medieval magicians was to turn ordinary metal into gold. In about 1450 Bernard of Treviso tried mixing 2,000 eggs with olive oil and sulphuric acid. He cooked this for a fortnight, added metal and produced . . . the world's biggest omelette! It was a failure. He fed it to his pigs. It was probably the best meal they'd ever had. Just as well, really, since it was the last meal they ever had. It poisoned them.

Of course the monks were superstitious, too. They believed that parts of saints' bodies that were preserved (called 'relics') could work miracles.

Rotten relics

1. Even a small monastery would have a collection of holy relics. Tavaux monastery in France had . . .

† the hair of St Peter
† wood from the manger in which Jesus was born
† material from the robe and the shoes of Jesus' mother, Mary
† a tooth of St Maurice
† part of St Radegonde's jawbone
† St John the Baptist's finger
† bones from St Bernard
† one of the stones used to stone St Stephen to death
† a piece of the stone on which Jesus stood as he ascended to heaven

Someone must have known they were fakes!

2. Others claimed to have the cloth that baby Jesus was wrapped in, one of his teeth, drops of his blood-stained sweat, a piece of bread chewed by him and the basket used in the miracle of the loaves and the fishes.

3. Two French cathedrals, Angers and Amiens, *both* claimed to have the head of John the Baptist. A monastery in Constantinople said they were *both* wrong, because *they* had it! Perhaps John the Baptist, being a saint, had three heads.

4. The monks of Conques smuggled one of their brothers into the monastery at Agen. He waited TEN YEARS to be appointed the guardian of a saint's body. When he finally got the job he stole the body and carried it off to Conques.

5. Two monks from France were more honest. They travelled to Rome and paid good money for the body of St Sebastian. They were cheated. They were given the body of some Roman emperor instead. It was placed proudly under the altar at the abbey. Unfortunately it exploded with bad gases smelling like rotten eggs.

6. At least the bones of St Thomas Aquinas were genuine. He stopped off at the monastery of Fossanuova to rest on a journey . . . and died. The Fossanuova monks couldn't believe their luck. They quickly cut off his head and boiled his body to be sure of keeping his bones.

7. St Romuald of Ravenna was terrified on a visit to France. He learned that there was a plot to kill him because his body would be worth much more dead than alive.

8. Wandering friars (and confidence tricksters posing as friars) made a lot of money by selling relics at fairs. Pigs provided the bones of saints and St Apollonia's teeth were greatly prized – she was the patron saint of dentists – it seems that when she died she left hundreds and hundreds of teeth! Henry VI of England (king at the time of Jeanne's battles) was said to have collected a ton of them. Henry did not believe they were fakes – the huge number were simply the result of a saintly miracle.

9. When Henry VIII formed his own Church in England, hundreds of Catholic relics were collected and burned on bonfires.

10. In the local church of Jeanne the Maid was a memorial to a young Christian who died for his faith. It was said that the man was beheaded – then picked up his head and gave a sermon with it before he died.

If medieval people could believe such incredible things, is it surprising that they believed a peasant girl could be a witch?

7 THE CLOTHES FILE

It seems strange to us that Jeanne the Maid was burned to death because she chose to wear men's clothes! In fact clothes were very important to medieval people.
Men and women were totally different, the Church said. It was a great crime for women to try to look like men . . . or for men to try to look like women!

Shoes and sins

We have to remember that in medieval times men were believed to be better human beings than women. Women were expected to obey their male relations. A husband had the right to beat his wife – but not if he was drunk or in a temper. According to a medieval Italian proverb: *A horse, whether good or bad, needs a spur. A woman, whether good or bad, needs a lord and master – and sometimes a stick.*

A travelling preacher, Robert d'Abrissel, went further. He said: *A woman is a witch, a snake, a plague, a rat, a rash, a poison, a burning flame and an assistant of the Devil.*

So the worst thing a man could do was to be like a woman. Two hundred years before Jeanne's birth monks were writing about men's dreadful fashions. They worried that men who wore colourful, fancy clothes were becoming more like women. That was a sin. So was . . .

Wearing shoes with pointed toes. Monk Oderic Vitalis had some very harsh words for Lord Fulk of Anjou. Lord Fulk's 'crime' was to invent shoes with long pointed toes that became a popular fashion. Spiteful Oderic said Fulk only wore them, "to hide the shape of his twisted feet which are covered in lumps we call bunions".

Wearing shoes with curly toes.
Pointed shoes came to have such long tips that young men had to chain the points to their knees so they did not trip over them! The Church said such shoes were sinful and called them 'devils' claws'.

A woman dressed as a knight. The church then turned its anger on women's fashion. In fourteenth-century England women who rode to tournaments looking more like knights than spectators were called evil. They were criticised for wearing tunics like knights and carrying daggers.

Wearing pointed hats. While Jeanne the Maid was riding to Charles's help a monk was also on the roads of northern France. His name was Thomas Couette. He went around preaching against the 'steeple' hats that ladies wore. He said they were a sign of the deadly sin of Pride and told them to wear humble peasant caps. They obeyed and burned the steeples . . . until Friar Thomas moved on somewhere else. Then the women went back to wearing taller steeples than ever!

Wearing platform shoes. Shoes raised up on platforms of cork were popular with ladies in Spain and Italy in Jeanne's day. Apart from being sinful, the monks said, they wasted cork and they wasted cloth – women needed more material to make the dresses reach the ground. Laws were passed to stop women wearing them.

Wearing clothes too fine for you. In many medieval countries laws were passed saying that only nobles could wear fine clothes. If you were a peasant you should not wear rich clothes – otherwise people would mistake you for something better!

The trouble was most peasants had no choice about what they could wear. The English poet William Langland described a peasant couple working in the fields in his poem **The Vision of Piers Plowman.**

The Peasants

His coat of a cloth that is thin as the east wind,
His hood full of holes with the hair sticking through,
His clumsy shoes, knobbled and nailed over thickly,
Yet his toes poked clean through as he trod on the ground.
Two miserable mittens made out of old rags,
The fingers worn out and the filth caked on them,
He waded in mud almost up to his ankles,
In front are four oxen, so weary and feeble
Their ribs could be counted, so wretched they were.
His wife walked beside him, and carried the ox whip,
She wore a poor cloth coat cut short to the knee,
Wrapped in a floor cloth to keep out the weather,
She was barefoot on bare ice, until her feet bled.
At the end of the furrow there lay a small bread-dish,
And in it their baby, all wrapped up in cloths,
And two more, just two years' old, at the far side,
And they all sang a song that was mournful to hear;
They cried out in voices so full of their sadness
The poor man sighed angrily, "Children, be still!"

Was this the sort of life a peasant girl like Ellie would have had to look forward to? Had Jeanne seen similar sights in the fields at Domremy? Was this why she refused marriage to the young man and preferred going to war?

Jeanne the Maid was given some quite fine clothes to wear when she was in Charles's company. Her judges tried to say that this was wrong — she shouldn't dress as a lady, she shouldn't dress as a man. She should dress as a peasant. The judges were also interested in how her angels dressed.

-89-

Part Three
The Truth About Jeanne

8

The journey back to Domremy passed like a dream. We were in no hurry. We stopped in small towns along the way where I traded prayers for food. Once I wrote a letter for a farmer and earned us comfortable beds for the night. Sometimes Ellie helped in a local inn as a pot girl and made a little money. Someone gave her a green dress. She bathed in the river and washed her hair before she put it on. "I've never had a proper dress before," she said with a strange shyness.

She changed in a barn. It was a different girl from the one who'd left Domremy a month before. Or perhaps it was a different monk who looked at her. Everything was so certain when I left the monastery. Each day in the monastery was like the day before. Prayers were said at the same times. "How boring!" Ellie said once. "In the countryside every day's different. Lambing, harvesting, plants growing and dying all the time. You never know what will happen next."

"Doesn't that scare you?" I asked.

She stopped in the middle of the road and looked at me. "Not as much as your Church scares me," she said. "If they can burn a woman for dressing like a man . . ."

"It's against God's law," I repeated.

"Yes? So how come it's all right for you monks to wear a dress, eh?"

"A dress? This is a habit. All monks wear habits. It's not a dress."

"Looks like a dress to me," she sniffed and marched down the road to Domremy, her green skirt swinging with every step.

I was miserable that day. My Church, my habit, my prayers – all the things that made me feel safe – began to seem different to me. Maybe it was Jeanne the Maid, maybe it was Ellie, but now nothing was certain.

"Cheer up," Ellie told me. "At least you can tell Madame du Lys about her daughter, can't you?"

The nearer we came to Domremy the more exciting that thought became. The fields around the farm were even more parched than when we left. Only the weeds were thriving. "My dad's too idle to keep the fields in order," Ellie sighed. "Since Monsieur du Lys died, and his sons left the farm, Dad doesn't have anyone to give him orders."

"What about Madame du Lys?" I asked.

Ellie sighed. "Johnny, you've seen the way men treat women. Men have no respect for women here."

"They respected Jeanne," I reminded her.

"Only while she was winning," Ellie retorted bitterly. "When she started losing they burned her."

"No they didn't!" I cried and hurried over the cobbled yard. I rattled on the kitchen door and heard that hollow echo again. Madame du Lys stepped from a barn with a small bag of flour she had been grinding. Her dress and hands were covered with a fine white dust. "Brother!" she said and almost smiled. "You have news of my daughter?"

"I have," I said, stepping forward.

The woman trembled and let herself sink onto a pile of straw. "Tell me . . . is she alive?"

I was just about to answer when a voice came from behind me. "Your daughter is alive, madame," Ellie said. I swung round. Her face was strangely serious. She knelt in

front of the woman and took her hand. She spoke softly and quickly.

"Catherine is still alive."

"Catherine?"

"Your daughter Catherine is alive and well. She's with your son Jacquemin in Orleans."

I think my mouth must have gaped like the village well. I could do nothing but listen to Ellie with wonder.

"What about Jeanne?" Madame du Lys implored.

"Jeanne is dead, madame. She lost a battle in the north and she was captured. They sold her to the English. The English had to get rid of her so they handed her over to the Church and told the Church to burn her. The Church gave her a sort of trial and could hardly find a good reason to have her executed. So they showed her death in a churchyard and that made her confess. Then they warned her not to wear men's clothing ever again."

"She fought in men's clothes," Madame du Lys sighed. "I was with Jeanne at Charles's coronation at Reims. She was wearing armour then. If it's good enough for a coronation it should be good enough for a prison."

"I think they may have taken Jeanne's dress away from her. They left her nothing but breeches and a tunic to wear. As soon as she put them on they had their excuse to burn her."

"I had hoped she might have been saved," the woman sighed. "God and his angels sent her to fight. She won the crown for King Charles . . ."

"They all deserted her at the end," Ellie said. She gave me a hard stare. "Even God and his angels."

Madame du Lys nodded slowly. "I thought it was too much to hope for. But what is Catherine doing in Orleans?"

"Pretending to be Jeanne," Ellie said. "I think it was probably Jacquemin's idea. As soon as Jeanne became a favourite of the king then her brothers joined her and became wealthy."

The woman nodded. "Even my husband made his fortune from Jeanne's fame," she said. "We were the simple Darc family once. Now we have the du Lys title."

"Maybe Jacquemin decided this farm was too much work. Maybe going back to Orleans with their heroine was a quick way to make money. The people gathered hundreds of pounds and gave them to Jacquemin and Catherine because they believed it was Jeanne returning."

"So Jacquemin dressed Catherine as Jeanne?" Madame du Lys asked.

I had to cut in, "What about Richard? Abbot Richard said it was Jeanne!"

"Abbot Richard always joined the winning side," Ellie said. "A few lies didn't matter to him . . . especially if it meant a share of Jacquemin's and Catherine's fortune."

"He's a monk!" I cried.

Ellie gave me that hard stare again. "No. He's only a man." She turned back to the silent Madame du Lys. "I'm sorry to bring you this news, madame, but I think it's best that you know the truth about Jeanne."

The woman nodded. "Yes. I can lay her to rest again in my mind. Jeanne was a strange child, but she was good. She really believed she heard those angel voices."

"I know," Ellie said and stood up. "Madame du Lys, will you tell my father and mother that I'm going back. Back to Orleans . . . maybe on to Paris. I've seen the town and it's exciting. I want to live there."

Madame du Lys smiled gently. "Good luck, and bless you."

Ellie strode across the yard and on to the road. To the west it led into the setting sun, back to Orleans. To the east it led towards the darkness and back to the monastery. I followed her to the gateway.

The red light lit her face and reflected in her eyes. "A man who can read and write can make a good living in the town," she said softly. "Or would you rather rot in your cold grey monastery?"

She didn't wait for an answer but turned and began walking slowly towards the sun, red as the witch-fire that my Church had lit under Jeanne.

I took one step after Ellie, then another . . . and I headed into the fire.

EPILOGUE

Over the years many fantastic stories have been woven around Jeanne the Maid – or Joan of Arc as she is better known.

In 1810 a historian tried to prove that Jeanne was in fact the secret sister of King Charles VII, that she was smuggled out of Paris to save her from her father's enemies. According to this story the Darc family at Domremy were her foster parents for sixteen years.

This story was repeated and became popular in a book published in 1965. The writer then went on to 'prove' that Jeanne escaped the execution and lived happily ever after with a husband. The main 'proof' was the appearance of Jeanne in Orleans in 1349 – eight years after her death. The historian completely ignored another piece of evidence because it didn't suit his story. This is it: the king invited the fake Jeanne to dinner. She failed to appear. Later she was arrested in Paris and confessed that she was not Jeanne the Maid.

Another historian argued that the fake was possibly Jeanne's sister – Catherine – and this is the idea used for the story of Ellie and John.

Whoever the fake was, it was almost certainly not Jeanne the Maid. She died a horrible death at the stake. She died because she dared to argue with the power of the Church. She died because she was a woman in a man's world.

She died . . . but not before she had changed that world. For ever.